Eye on Energy

Everyday Conservation

ABDO
Publishing Company

Jill C. Wheeler

Published by ABDO Publishing Company, 8000 West 78th Street, Edina, Minnesota 55439.
Copyright © 2008 by Abdo Consulting Group, Inc. International copyrights reserved in all
countries. No part of this book may be reproduced in any form without written permission from
the publisher. The Checkerboard Library™ is a trademark and logo of ABDO Publishing Company.

Printed in the United States.

Cover Photo: Getty Images
Interior Photos: Alamy p. 23; AP Images p. 27; Corbis pp. 7, 14-15, 18, 19, 20, 22, 25, 26, 29;
    Getty Images pp. 6, 9, 10, 11, 12, 13, 17, 21, 28; Ken Lax/Photo Researchers, Inc. p. 5;
    Peter Arnold p. 4; U.S. Department of Energy p. 17

Series Coordinator: Rochelle Baltzer
Editors: Rochelle Baltzer, BreAnn Rumsch
Art Direction & Cover Design: Neil Klinepier

Library of Congress Cataloging-in-Publication Data

Wheeler, Jill C., 1964-
 Everyday conservation / Jill C. Wheeler.
    p. cm. – (Eye on energy)
 Includes index.
 ISBN 978–1–59928–804–8
 1. Energy conservation–Juvenile literature. I. Title.

TJ163.35.W44 2007
333.72–dc22

2007007112

CONTENTS

SIMPLE STEPS

Many people are talking about new and different energy sources. Likewise, scientists are researching how more energy can be obtained for the world's rising population.

Yet, creating more energy is only one plan for addressing the growing energy demand. Another option is making thoughtful choices about ways to use less energy. This idea is called energy conservation.

Conserving energy might not seem very exciting. Some people worry that life won't be as pleasant

Large cities, such as New York City, New York, use a lot of energy. As populations continue to grow, conserving energy becomes more important.

if they use less energy. Yet, that's not always true. There are many ways to conserve energy. Some methods impose substantial lifestyle changes. But, many approaches lead to very little change.

For example, your family could switch to more **efficient** lightbulbs. Purchasing and **installing** new lightbulbs takes time and money.

Recycling can save energy! It almost always takes less energy to make a product from recycled materials than from new materials. For example, using recycled aluminum cans to make new cans uses 95 percent less energy than using new aluminum.

But after that, your lives probably won't be any different. And, your parents will notice a lower electricity bill!

Unlike coal power plants, nuclear plants do not emit carbon dioxide. However, they generate dangerous waste.

Conserving energy can make a major difference for the **environment**. In the 1970s, California began requiring home **appliances** to be more **efficient**. Because of this action, the state has avoided building more than 20 power plants! That means California now has much less **greenhouse gas emissions** or nuclear waste than it could have had.

In 1992, Minnesota started its Conservation Improvement Program. The program charges consumers a little extra money each month for electricity and natural gas. Utility companies, which supply these types of power, collect the extra money. Then, they use it to reward consumers who purchase energy-efficient appliances.

Since its start, Minnesota's program has saved more than 2,000 **megawatts** of power. That's the same amount of power that two nuclear power plants generate. Because of the program, those plants did not need to be built. Likewise, no one needed to figure out where to store the nuclear waste.

Riding a bicycle is a fun way to conserve energy!

Conservation alone will not solve the world's energy problems. Yet, it can reduce the problem. This makes the growing energy demand easier to address. In fact, one expert believes that if all states had programs like California's and Minnesota's, there would be major benefits. The United States could reduce the amount of energy it's expected to use in the next ten years by half!

FACT OR FICTION?

The United States uses the most energy in the world.

Fact. The average American consumes five times as much energy as the average global citizen.

WHY CONSERVE?

Most of the time, energy sources involve both advantages and disadvantages. For example, nuclear power does not **emit greenhouse gases**, such as **carbon dioxide**, that lead to **global warming**. But, it produces waste that can be deadly to living things.

In contrast, energy conservation usually involves more advantages than disadvantages. For example, most electricity in the United States is generated from burning coal. Therefore, using less electricity means less coal is burned. So by turning off a light you don't need, you are helping reduce greenhouse gas emissions!

People can also conserve energy by using less gasoline. You can choose to walk to a store, instead of asking someone to drive you there. This decision means no greenhouse gases are emitted. Walking might take longer, but it is good for your body. You can exercise and help curb global warming at the same time!

Conserving energy usually costs less than using energy. For example, it costs less to not use a light than to use one. And, it costs less to not fly on an airplane than to take a flight. In addition, many businesses conserve energy to avoid paying for unnecessary power.

Some people turn away from energy-saving devices because they often cost more to purchase. For example, **hybrid** cars are more expensive than regular cars. And, compact fluorescent lightbulbs cost more than regular, or incandescent, lightbulbs. But over time, these energy-conservation helpers pay for themselves in energy savings.

Walking instead of driving saves energy and helps the environment. Plus, it's good exercise!

ENERGY UPGRADES

Advances in technology have helped the quest to save energy. Most of these allow people to more **efficiently** accomplish their tasks. The compact fluorescent lightbulb is one such advancement.

Inside an incandescent lightbulb, there is a thin, coiled wire called a filament. When a light switch is flipped on, an **electric current** flows through the filament in the lightbulb. It heats the filament to more than 4,500 degrees Fahrenheit (2,480°C)! The extreme temperature makes the filament give off light. However, using heat to create light is not very efficient.

Incandescent lightbulb

Compact fluorescent lightbulbs work differently. They consist of a glass tube that contains a small amount of **mercury** vapor and a chemically inactive gas. When an electric current flows through the tube, it causes the mercury vapor to give off **ultraviolet** light. The inside of the tube is coated with

ENERGY BUZZ
In February 2007, Australia announced its plan to ban incandescent lightbulbs. The bulbs will be phased out by 2010 and replaced with compact fluorescent lightbulbs. Australia is the first country to do this. The state of California has also proposed the idea.

chemicals that give off visible light when struck by **ultraviolet** rays.

Compact fluorescent lightbulbs create much less heat than incandescent lightbulbs. As a result, they are far more **efficient**. That is why a 15-**watt** fluorescent lightbulb produces as much light as a 60-watt incandescent lightbulb.

Try replacing 25 percent of your home's lightbulbs in high-use areas with compact fluorescent lightbulbs. Your family could save about 50 percent on lighting bills!

Improvements are also being made in the way electricity moves from a power plant to your house. Usually, electricity travels a far distance to its **destination**. Along the way, some electrical energy is lost. That is due to resistance, which opposes **electric currents**. Less electricity reaches the ending point because resistance turns some of the electric energy into heat.

The electricity your toaster uses travels a long way to toast your bread!

For many years, scientists have known that much of this energy could be saved by chilling metal power lines. Less energy is lost when electric currents travel through extremely cold metal. But, getting the power lines cold enough has been the problem. Generally, they must be below -253 degrees Fahrenheit (-158°C).

New technologies today use special materials and liquid **nitrogen** to chill power lines. Without resistance, these power lines can carry up to 200 times as much power as regular cables. One test of these chilled cables began in May 2006 in Albany, New York. If the test is successful, the U.S. Department of Energy hopes to **upgrade** the U.S. power grid with the cables by 2030.

Officials see the United States as a promising place for new technology in power lines. This is because much of the country's power grid was constructed in the 1960s and needs upgrading anyway. Aging power lines have been blamed for large-scale blackouts in parts of the country.

EFFICIENT LIVING

Most people use more energy at home than anywhere else. That energy is usually in the form of electricity or natural gas. Homes use this energy to heat and cool rooms, to heat water, and to power electronic devices.

Experts say it's fairly easy for people to cut their home energy bills by about 30 percent. Some conservation methods are simple. For example, it's easy to switch off the lights when you leave a room. And, it's easy to latch the door when you come in from outside.

You can even go one step further. Ask your parents to use only compact fluorescent lightbulbs. These lightbulbs use 70 percent less energy than incandescent lightbulbs! And, they last about 10,000 hours. Standard lightbulbs only last about 750 hours.

You can make a big difference by being on the lookout for things that use power even when they are turned off. These devices are called "energy vampires." For example, if you see a cellular-phone charger plugged in with no phone attached, unplug it. It's using energy even when it's not charging anything.

Be sure to turn off computers, televisions, and lights that are not in use. Even better, plug electronic devices into a power strip. That way, the strip can easily be switched on and off, so the devices do not become energy vampires.

Your parents can also trim their energy costs by using **appliances** that are energy **efficient**. Energy experts say that if Americans do this, the United States could avoid building many new power plants.

Energy-efficient appliances save owners money, too. For example, refrigerators that were made before 1993 cost about $140 per year to run. A new Energy Star refrigerator uses only about $20 in electricity per year!

Your family can also conserve energy by setting the **thermostat** to 65 degrees Fahrenheit (18°C) at night. Even better, urge your family to purchase a programmable thermostat. This type of thermostat **automatically** turns down the temperature at night or when no one is home. It can also be set to automatically raise the temperature so the house is cozy when you return.

Don't forget to conserve energy during holidays, too. Ask your parents to buy light-**emitting** diode (LED) holiday lights instead of regular incandescent holiday lights.

Standard holiday lights produce heat that is wasted. In contrast, LED lights generate very little heat. LED lights are specially designed so that more energy goes directly toward generating light. In fact, they use up to 99 percent less energy than regular holiday lights!

ENERGY STAR

Energy Star is the symbol of energy efficiency. Its logo is labeled on products that use the most energy-efficient technologies. These products must meet standards set by the U.S. Department of Energy and the U.S. Environmental Protection Agency. The Energy Star program began in 1992 and is backed by the U.S. government.

Energy Star aims to reduce both pollution and energy bills. Some Energy Star home products include clothes washers, refrigerators, dishwashers, televisions, VCRs, and lights.

Energy Star clothes washers use about 35 to 50 percent less water than regular washers. And, they monitor water temperature to conserve hot water. Also, washers spin clothes better so they take less time in dryers. Overall, Energy Star clothes washers use 50 percent less energy per load than regular washers.

Your family probably cannot replace all of your home appliances at once. However, it makes sense to consider buying an Energy Star model when an appliance needs to be replaced. In fact, if just one in every ten households bought Energy Star-rated appliances, the change would be the same as planting 1.7 million new trees!

Using an Energy Star clothes washer can save more than 9,440 gallons (35,730 L) of water per year in every household. That's more water than the average person drinks in a lifetime!

ELECTRONIC ENERGY

Chances are, your grandparents did not worry much about saving energy when they were young. Most of their toys probably did not use electricity. But, many popular toys today use a lot of energy. Anything that plugs into an outlet to operate or to recharge uses electricity.

For example, computers use electricity. You may use them for schoolwork or to play games. When computers are not in use, they can be turned off or put in sleep mode. But, they still use some energy in sleep mode. To save energy, turn computers all the way off.

Your family can also conserve energy by purchasing televisions that are energy **efficient**. Big-screen televisions are very popular, but they use more electricity than smaller televisions. Experts estimate that

by 2009, U.S. televisions will use about 50 percent more electricity than they currently use. This is mostly because so many people are switching to larger televisions.

Each year, U.S. televisions use about the same amount of electricity needed to power all the homes in the state of New York!

Make one afternoon every week a "power's off" time. Exploring outside uses no electricity, and you never know what you may find!

Don't worry, you don't have to give up watching television and playing video games to save energy. Instead, ask your parents to plug the television into a power strip. When the television is not in use, switch off the power strip. This stops it from being an energy vampire.

Better yet, turn off the television and the computer. Minimal light is needed to read a book or to play a board game. And, playing games outside during the day requires no light. You can save energy and still have fun!

WORLD ON WHEELS

Getting people and things from place to place uses a lot of energy and money. In 2005, the average U.S. household spent nearly $3,000 just to fuel two cars. Fortunately, there are ways to reduce these costs. Even if you don't drive, you can remind the drivers in your family how to save energy on the road.

Challenge your family to avoid one car trip per week. Walk, bicycle, or take mass **transit** if possible. Or, share a ride with someone. If you ride a school bus, you already do this. Adults can also do this by carpooling with other adults to work or to other activities.

There are ways to conserve energy when driving, too. Obeying the speed limit saves energy. Cars are

In response to an oil shortage in 1973, the United States adopted the 55 miles-per-hour (89 km/h) speed limit. But in 1987, Congress allowed states to increase speed limits on rural interstates to 65 miles per hour (105 km/h). Starting in 1995, states became allowed to set their own speed limits.

designed to drive most **efficiently** at about 60 miles per hour (97 km/h). For each five miles per hour (8 km/h) over that speed, efficiency can decrease up to 23 percent.

Drivers should also take off from stoplights and stop signs at a moderate pace. Lightning-fast starts and abrupt stops can lower gas **mileage** by as much as 33 percent.

There are rewards for making energy-wise choices. On many highways, special lanes are reserved for people who carpool or drive hybrid cars.

You can also urge the drivers in your family to combine errands in one trip. Multistop trips with a warm engine can use half the gasoline of several short trips taken from cold starts. And, don't overload your family's vehicles. Extra weight reduces gas **mileage**.

What if you can't walk, bicycle, or take mass **transit** to your **destination**? Your family can still save energy by driving a fuel-**efficient** vehicle. If all U.S. cars could travel four more miles per gallon, the country could cut its gasoline demand by 15 percent! Technology exists to increase fuel efficiency by that amount. But unless those types of cars are in demand, automakers may be unwilling to spend the extra money that is needed to make them.

Ask your family members to run all of their errands at once. That way, they can save energy by avoiding multiple car trips.

City planners can help with energy conservation, too. As a city grows, people move farther away from the city center. This is called urban sprawl. It causes a lot more driving. City planners can limit how spread out a city becomes. That way, traveling around the city can remain efficient.

Even if city planners do not control urban sprawl, people can usually choose where they live. Living closer to where they work, meet friends, attend school, and worship helps the **environment**.

In urban areas, many people take public transportation, such as subways or buses. In New York City, New York, more than 4 million people ride the city's subway system every day.

SAVING AT SCHOOL

Like homes and businesses, schools also use plenty of energy. In fact, many schools spend more of their budget on energy than they spend on textbooks. It makes sense for schools to conserve energy and use their money for other important things. There are several ways students can help their schools use less energy.

Just as you do at home, turn off lights in rooms that are not in use. Lighting accounts for about 19 percent of the energy used in most schools. Tell your school staff members to use energy-saving compact fluorescent lightbulbs, too.

And if your classroom is drafty, there are ways to help without turning up the heat. Ask your teacher to conduct a class experiment to find out where the drafts come in. If doors and windows do not shut completely, stuff the cracks with suitable **insulation**. You could make long, thin cloth bags stuffed with beans or fabric scraps to use as insulation. That will help reduce your school's heating bill.

Don't forget to help your school save energy! Form a light patrol with your friends to make sure the lights are turned off at the end of each school day.

Turning off one typical computer at night and on weekends can save more than $30 annually. So, a school with 100 computers could save $3,000 a year!

Keep an eye on school computers, too. Turn them all the way off at the end of each day. Do the same for televisions, DVD players, and VCRs. And, watch for chargers that are plugged into outlets but are not charging anything. Ask school staff members to turn printers and fax machines all the way off, too.

For another project, walk around your school and make a list of all the things that use electricity. Ask the school staff if all of those things are necessary. Is there is an old refrigerator with very little in it? See if it would be possible to move the contents to a newer refrigerator and unplug the old one.

PROJECT SPOTLIGHT

GREEN SCHOOLS PROGRAM

The Green Schools Program encourages schools to use less energy. The program also teaches students how to conserve energy at home and in their communities. In addition, it saves schools money on energy costs.

WHO: The Green Schools Program is managed by the Alliance to Save Energy, located in Washington, D.C.

Ask a staff member at your school if vending machine timers can be purchased to save energy.

TIMELINE: The program began in 1996. Currently, it is active in about 200 schools in select districts in California, Maryland, New York, New Jersey, North Carolina, and Pennsylvania.

HOW IT WORKS: The Green Schools Program gives grants to school districts to help them start energy-conservation programs. Schools agree to put the money they save back into the school.

ACTIVITIES: Participating schools have found many ways to save energy. One school installed timers on their vending machines. Now, the machines turn off when school is not in session. The school also unplugs all of its computers during Thanksgiving and Christmas vacations to avoid using standby power. Another school saved more than $3,000 in energy costs in one year. It used the savings to replace all of the regular lightbulbs with compact fluorescent lightbulbs throughout the community.

GET INVOLVED: To get your school involved, visit the Green Schools Program Web site at www.ase.org/section/program/greenschl.

BUILDING SMART

The buildings we live and work in use about 40 percent of all the energy consumed in the United States. So, it makes sense to make those buildings as **efficient** as possible. Experts say new efficient buildings use 70 percent less energy than older buildings.

For example, there have been improvements in home heating and cooling methods. Heat pumps obtain natural heat from underground to warm homes. And, white metal roofs make use of the sun's heat. Home builders may also determine how to best position a home to capture solar heat.

Solar panels collect heat from sunlight. They transfer it to air or water flowing through tubes behind the panel. This heat may be used directly or stored for later use.

Some builders are creating Zero-Energy Homes (ZEHs). These homes have solar panels, which generate electricity. And, they have special windows that block solar heat in the summer and retain indoor warmth in the winter. They also feature compact fluorescent lightbulbs. And, they have a special water heater that warms water only when a faucet is running.

ZEHs may cost around $25,000 more than similar homes without energy-saving additions. However, the U.S. Department of Energy hopes to eliminate those extra costs by 2020.

New technologies have emerged over time. They make conserving energy easier and more convenient. But in the end, it is each person's responsibility to make smart decisions about saving energy. The more energy people save today, the more energy there will be for future generations.

THIS HOUSE USES
80% LESS ENERGY
THAN THE AVERAGE HOME

The BASF Near-Zero Energy Home-Paterson, N.J.

Built as part of the BASF Better Home, Better Planet Initiative, this house demonstrates the benefits of high-performance materials using chemistry. It is stronger, faster to build, more affordable to own and has a lower impact on the environment.

After the demonstration phase, this home will be donated to St. Michael's Housing Corporation.

Learn more: www.betterhomebetterplanet.com

Helping Make Buildings Better™

□ · BASF
The Chemical Company

ZEHs are a step toward an environmentally friendly world. Plus, owners of these homes save a substantial amount of money in electricity costs. For example, one ZEH in Tennessee runs completely on electricity for just eighty-two cents a day. In comparison, conventional homes nearby use between four and five dollars in electricity daily.

GLOSSARY

appliance - a household or office device operated by gas or electric current. Common kitchen appliances include a stove, a refrigerator, and a dishwasher.

automatic - happening by itself, without anyone's control.

carbon dioxide - a heavy, fireproof, colorless gas that is formed when fuel containing the element carbon is burned.

destination - the place that someone or something is going to.

efficient - the ability to produce a desired result, especially without wasting time or energy.

electric current - a flow of electric charge.

emit - to give off or out. An emission is something that has been emitted.

environment - all the surroundings that affect the growth and well-being of a living thing.

global warming - an increase in the average temperature of Earth's surface.

greenhouse gas - a gas, such as carbon dioxide, that traps heat in the atmosphere.

hybrid - combining two or more functions or ways of operation. For example, gasoline-electric hybrid cars run on both gasoline and electric power.

install - to set up something for use.

insulation - material used to keep something from losing or transferring electricity, heat, or sound.

megawatt - one million watts.

mercury - a silver white metallic element, which is one of the more than 100 basic substances that have atoms of only one kind. Mercury is used in batteries and various scientific instruments.

mileage - the average number of miles a motor vehicle can travel per gallon of gasoline.

nitrogen - a colorless, odorless, tasteless gas that is the most plentiful element in Earth's atmosphere and is found in all living matter.

thermostat - a device for regulating temperature in a home or other building.

transit - the moving of persons or things from one place to another.

ultraviolet - a type of light that cannot be seen with the human eye.

upgrade - to increase or improve.

watt - a unit of electric power that equals the work done at the rate of one joule per second.

WEB SITES

To learn more about energy conservation, visit ABDO Publishing Company on the World Wide Web at **www.abdopublishing.com**. Web sites about energy conservation are featured on our Book Links page. These links are routinely monitored and updated to provide the most current information available.

INDEX